D1541769

DISCOVER ☙ DOGS WITH
THE AMERICAN CANINE ASSOCIATION

AMERICAN CANINE ASSOCIATION, INC.
ACA
OFFICIAL SEAL

❤ ❤ ❤ ❤ ❤ ❤ **I LIKE** ❤ ❤ ❤ ❤ ❤ ❤

POODLES!

Linda Bozzo

It is the Mission of the American Canine Association (ACA) to provide registered dog owners with the educational support needed for raising, training, showing, and breeding the healthiest pets expected by responsible pet owners throughout the world. Through our activities and services, we encourage and support the dog world in order to promote best-known husbandry standards as well as to ensure that the voice and needs of our customers are quickly and properly addressed.

Our continued support, commitment, and direction are guided by our customers, including veterinary, legal, and legislative advisors. ACA aims to provide the most efficient, cooperative, and courteous service to our customers and strives to set the standard for education and problem solving for all who depend on our services.

For more information, please visit www.acacanines.com, e-mail customerservice@acadogs.com, phone 1-800-651-8332, or write to the American Canine Association at PO Box 121107, Clermont, FL 34712.

Enslow Elementary, an imprint of Enslow Publishers, Inc.

Enslow Elementary® is a registered trademark of Enslow Publishers, Inc.

Library of Congress Cataloging-in-Publication Data

Bozzo, Linda.
  I like poodles! / Linda Bozzo.
    p. cm. — (Discover dogs with the American Canine Association)
  Includes bibliographical references and index.
  Summary: "Early readers will learn how to care for a poodle, including breed-specific traits and needs"—Provided by publisher.
  ISBN 978-0-7660-3850-9
  1. Poodles—Juvenile literature. I. Title.
SF429.P85.B69 2012
636.72'8—dc22
                        2011010477

Future editions:
Paperback ISBN 978-1-4644-0118-3
ePUB ISBN 978-1-4645-1025-0
PDF ISBN 978-1-4646-1025-7

Printed in the United States of America

012012 The HF Group, North Manchester, IN

10 9 8 7 6 5 4 3 2 1

To Our Readers: We have done our best to make sure all Internet Addresses in this book were active and appropriate when we went to press. However, the author and the publisher have no control over and assume no liability for the material available on those Internet sites or on other Web sites they may link to. Any comments or suggestions can be sent by e-mail to comments@enslow.com or to the address on the back cover.

Every effort has been made to locate all copyright holders of material used in this book. If any errors or omissions have occurred, corrections will be made in future editions of this book.

Photo Credits: Angelika Fischer/Photos.com, p. 13 (hamburger); Annette Shaff/Photos.com, p. 13 (collar); © Chico Sanchez/Alamy, p. 18; Debi Bishop/Photos.com, p. 3 (left); Eddie Green/Photos.com, p. 23; © iStockphoto.com/Janalynn, p. 14; jclegg/Photos.com, p. 13 (leash and rope); © Jean Michel Labat/ardea.com, p. 13 (poodle); Marina Maslennikova/Photos.com, p. 7; Shutterstock.com, pp. 1, 3 (right), 5, 6, 8, 10, 11,13 (bed, bowls, brush), 17, 19, 21; Yangfei Wu/Photos.com, p. 9.

Cover Photo: Marina Maslennikova/Photos.com (brown poodle).

Enslow Elementary
an imprint of
Enslow Publishers, Inc.
40 Industrial Road
Box 398
Berkeley Heights, NJ 07922
USA
http://www.enslow.com

CONTENTS

IS A POODLE RIGHT FOR YOU?

Poodles come in three sizes: **standard** (large), **miniature** (medium), and **toy** (small). Because a toy poodle is so small, it is not the right dog for very young children. They may hurt the little toy poodles by accident.

Poodles are smart so you can teach them to do tricks. They make great pets!

Poodles are good with children and other pets.

Puppies are full of energy. Can your family keep up?

A DOG OR PUPPY?

Poodle puppies are easy to train.
But they still need lots of attention.
An older dog may already be trained.
Does your family have the
time to train and take
care of a puppy?

LOVING YOUR POODLE

Take time every day to love
your poodle. Teach him
new tricks. Play with
your poodle and he will
love you back.

Your poodle will love being with you.

Running and playing keep poodles healthy.

EXERCISE

Poodles like to keep busy. They enjoy long walks on a **leash** and they like to play. Did you know that poodles are also good swimmers?

Poodles were born to swim!

FEEDING YOUR POODLE

Poodles can be fed wet or dry dog food. Ask a **veterinarian (vet)**, a doctor for animals, which food to feed your dog and how much to feed her. Give your poodle fresh, clean water every day.

Remember to keep your dog's food and water dishes clean. Dirty dishes can make her sick.

Do not feed your poodle people food. It can make her sick.

Your new dog will need:

a collar with a tag

a bed

a brush

food and water dishes

a leash

toys

A groomer cuts a poodle's hair.

GROOMING

Your poodle will need his hair cut by a **groomer** often. Since poodles hardly **shed**, most people are not allergic to them. A poodle can be bathed every six weeks. Bathe your poodle with gentle soap made just for dogs.

You also need to clip your dog's nails. A vet or groomer can show you how.

WHAT YOU SHOULD KNOW

Poodles are good watchdogs, so they enjoy barking. You will want to train your poodle not to bark too much.

A healthy poodle is known to live as long as fourteen years. The toy and miniature poodles generally live longer than the standard poodles.

Poodles like to watch what is going on around them.

You will need to take your new dog to the vet for a checkup. He will need shots, called vaccinations, and yearly checkups to keep him healthy. If you think your dog may be sick or hurt, call your vet.

A GOOD FRIEND

Your poodle will be a very good friend. Play with her, feed her, and take good care of her. This will bring both of you many years of joy!

FUN FACT:
The poodle is the national dog of France.

NOTE TO PARENTS

It is important to consider having your dog spayed or neutered when the dog is young. Spaying and neutering are operations that prevent unwanted puppies and can help improve the overall health of your dog.

It is also a good idea to microchip your dog, in case he or she gets lost. A vet will implant a microchip under the skin that contains your contact information, which can then be scanned at a vet's office or animal shelter.

Some towns require licenses for dogs, so be sure to check with your town clerk.

For more information, speak with a vet.

There are many dogs, young and old, waiting to be adopted from animal shelters and rescue groups.

Words to Know

groomer—A person who cuts a dog's fur and nails.

leash—A chain or strap that connects to a dog's collar.

miniature—Smaller than the normal size.

shed—When a dog's hair falls out so new hair can grow.

standard—The normal size of a type of dog.

toy—The smallest size of dog.

vaccination—A shot that dogs need to stay healthy.

veterinarian (vet)—A doctor for animals.

Books

Gagne, Tammy. *Poodles.* Mankato, Minn.:
Capstone Press, 2010.

Landau, Elaine. *Poodles Are the Best!*
Minneapolis, Minn.: Lerner, 2010.

Mathea, Heidi. *Poodles.* Edina, Minn.:
ABDO Pub. Co., 2011.

Internet Addresses

American Canine Association Inc., Kids Corner
<http://acakids.com/>

Janet Wall's How to Love Your Dog: The Poodle
<http://loveyourdog.com/poodles.html>

INDEX